Being Kind During a Pandemic

by Brienna Rossiter

FOCUS
READERS®

PIONEER

www.focusreaders.com

Focus Readers is distributed by North Star Editions:
sales@northstareditions.com | 888-417-0195

Produced for Focus Readers by Red Line Editorial.

Photographs ©: Shutterstock Images, cover, 1, 4, 7, 9, 10, 12, 14, 16, 18, 20

Library of Congress Cataloging-in-Publication Data
Library of Congress Cataloging-in-Publication Data is available on the Library of Congress website.

ISBN
978-1-64493-680-1 (hardcover)
978-1-64493-716-7 (paperback)
978-1-64493-788-4 (ebook pdf)
978-1-64493-752-5 (hosted ebook)

Printed in the United States of America
Mankato, MN
012021

About the Author

Brienna Rossiter is a writer and editor who lives in Minnesota. She loves cooking food and being outside.

Table of Contents

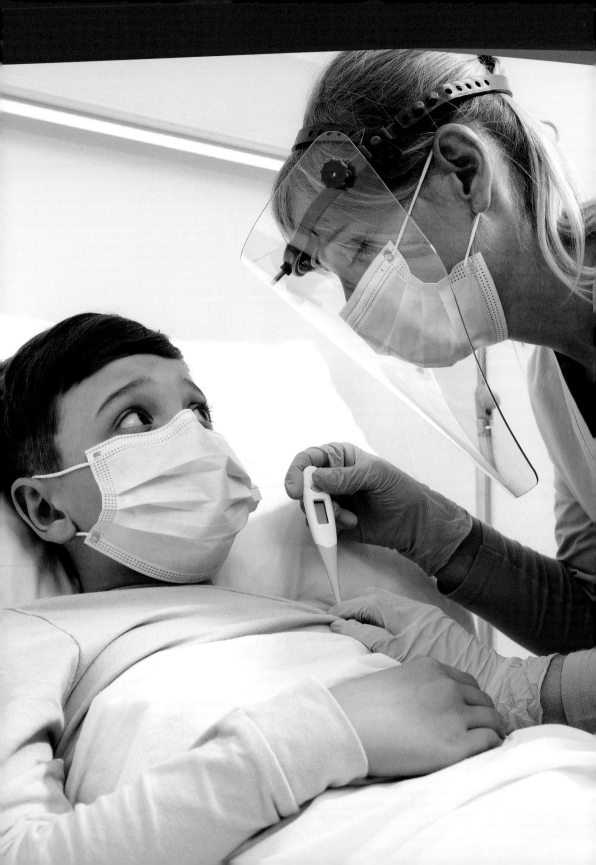

Chapter 1

Staying Safe

A **pandemic** is when an illness spreads very quickly. Many people get sick. Illnesses are caused by **germs**. If fewer germs spread, fewer people get sick.

You can help stop germs from spreading. Most germs spread from person to person. If you stay home more often, you will spread fewer germs. You will help others stay healthy. Keeping **distance** can also help.

Stopping Germs

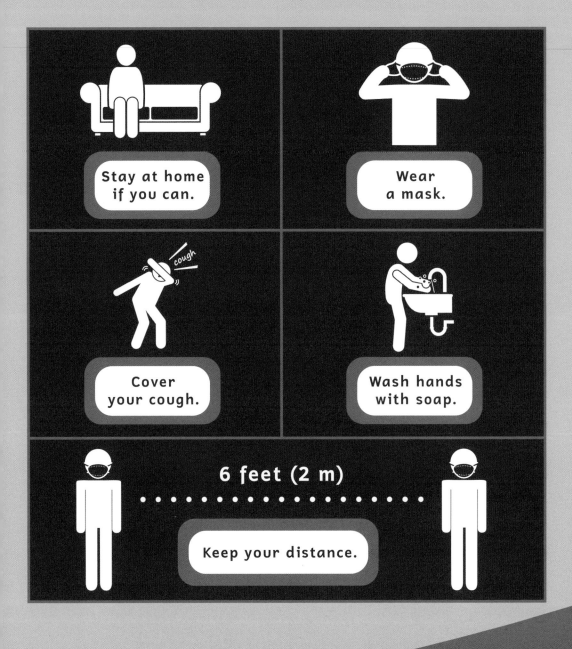

Stay at home if you can.

Wear a mask.

Cover your cough.

cough

Wash hands with soap.

6 feet (2 m)

Keep your distance.

Wash Your Hands

People get germs on their hands. So, wash your hands often. Always use soap. Soap helps get rid of germs. Spread the soap over all your fingers. Cover the backs of your hands, too. Rub your hands together for 20 seconds. Then **rinse** them off.

Chapter 2

Wear a Mask

Breathing in germs is one way that people get sick. You can help others by wearing a mask. A mask goes on your face. Make sure it covers your mouth and nose.

Masks trap germs that you breathe out. Masks stop germs from coughs. They stop germs from sneezes. When you wear a mask, you are less likely to make other people sick.

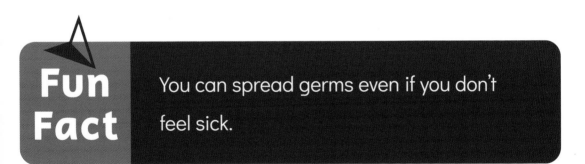

Fun Fact

You can spread germs even if you don't feel sick.

Chapter 3

Keep Your Distance

Germs spread faster when people are close together. You can show kindness by keeping your distance. Stay 6 feet (2 m) away from others. Also, do things outside if you can.

Germs spread more easily indoors. If you go into a store, wear a mask. And wash your hands when you get home. By changing your **behavior**, you can help keep other people safe.

Fun Fact

It's harder to keep your distance in a big group. So, try to keep groups small.

Chapter 4

Show Support

People can help one another while staying apart. They can meet outdoors. They can talk from far apart. They can drop off food for older people.

People can also find other ways to **connect**. They can talk on the phone. They can video chat. They can have classes online.

Being Kind During a Pandemic

Write your answers on a separate piece of paper.

1. Write a sentence explaining what a pandemic is.

2. Would you rather talk on the phone or do a video chat? Why?

3. How does wearing masks help people spread fewer germs?
    A. Masks block germs that people breathe out.
    B. Masks kill germs.
    C. Masks make germs harder to see.

4. What is an example of keeping your distance?
    A. giving hugs to many people at a party
    B. sitting close to friends on the same couch
    C. sitting outside in chairs that are far apart

Answer key on page 24.

Glossary

behavior
The way a person acts.

connect
To come together or feel close to one another.

distance
Space between yourself and other people.

germs
Tiny living things that can cause illness.

pandemic
When an illness spreads quickly to many people around the world.

parades
When groups of people walk or drive down a street in a long line, often to celebrate a person or event.

rinse
To run water over something, often to wash off dirt or soap.

To Learn More

BOOKS

Dolbear, Emily. *How Can I Help During COVID-19?* Mankato, MN: The Child's World, 2020.

Murray, Julie. *Staying Safe with Healthy Habits.* Minneapolis: Abdo Publishing, 2020.

NOTE TO EDUCATORS

Visit **www.focusreaders.com** to find lesson plans, activities, links, and other resources related to this title.

Index

Answer Key: **1.** Answers will vary; **2.** Answers will vary; **3.** A; **4.** C